Deputy for Christ

A Working Journal & Guide

For

Spiritual Warfare &

Awareness

By

Andrea M. Davis

Deputy for Christ: A Working Journal & Guide for Spiritual Warfare & Awareness

Table of Contents

Dedication

I would like to dedicate this book, first, to my God. Without God, I would not have the ability to write this book. I would not have the wherewithal to develop the words to write this devotional. I am grateful and thankful to God for the strength that He has given me to learn how to endure the hardships. I am thankful to God that He has taught me how to endure.

I dedicate this book to my children: Ayvori', E'lisia, Patrisha, Gabriel, and Delsyn are truly gifts sent from heaven. They have been with me throughout some hectic situations and never once judged me. They have loved me unconditionally and stood by my side. They have motivated me and been my strength through some tough times. They are my smile, my joy, and my laughter.

I dedicate this book to my parents, Andre, Sylvia, and Canese. All my parents have taught me the importance of survival. They have taught me the do's and don'ts of life and for that I am eternally grateful. My stepmother taught me how to pray and love God with all my heart. My father taught me how to get through the tough times by holding on, and consistently loving your family even when you face adversity. My biological mother, Canese, has taught me that despite what you experience you can overcome your past. My biological mother has experienced so many things, and has become a true soldier for the Lord.

This book is dedicated to my leader, Dr. Bishop Mary L. Alexander. She is been a mother, a friend, my confidant, my sister, my aunt, my cousin, my girlfriend. She has been whatever I have needed her to be. She has worked with me through all my foolishness and never made me feel like I could not make it. I am thankful for her life and consistent and persistent faith. She is truly an inspiration in my life.

I am thankful for my friends, sisters, and most of all family that have supported me throughout my life. I have been through changes and difficulties and those who know have been there for me and been consistent in their love and friendship.

~*Preface*~

I have spent many years hiding and running from my goals. Living with the thought that I would never do anything right or accomplish any goals I set out to do. I lived with regrets still while accomplishing goals simply to say to naysayers, "I am smart enough, beautiful enough, and I can accomplish anything despite your negative view of me."

My life changed over time and I have experienced many trials and tribulations. Although some childhood and adult experiences were rough, there was always an innate desire to become someone great. I knew at the age of eleven I would be someone great in God as I watched an evangelist preach. I told myself I would be her someday. I was saved by the age of 15 and my father and stepmother made sure we stayed in church. It was not until I became a divorced single mother of three that I recognized and experienced the presence of God. Now, a single mother of five I truly know God and have experienced Him repeatedly. Trust me, it will never get old.

I have lived through sexual abuse, abandonment, domestic abuse, persecution, depression, oppression, promiscuity, being taken advantage of, poor relationships, and so many worldly issues I could write three or four novels. I began writing my book in 2006. In 2014, I still only had one chapter. God would always have me write so many things, and I was always afraid to do something with what He gave me. I watched other women begin their ministries and take on the opportunities God gave them to reach the souls that were allotted to their hands. I would often tell myself, what could I say different, so I sat and did nothing. I downgraded myself, sat on my goals, and watched others press forward.

I spent the majority of my life trying to survive and taking care of my children. I lost some of myself along the way. Life was about survival and never about creating and attaining goals. I would go to school to have a better job, but not to accomplish creating a legacy that would move through the generations of my children, and my children's children. At some point, life had to shift, my thinking had to shift, and I had to begin to solidify my ministry and place in God. There was and is a remnant I have to reach.

Please understand that this book has only one purpose and that is to encourage a God-balanced life. Please ensure that you are making decisions that are best for you and your circumstances. I am only speaking to how God has brought me up and out and into a place of victorious living. My expectation is that you only see this as a guide to provoke positive thoughts and rejuvenate your ability to speak life for you, your situation, and your family.

Finally, I have taken all of the thoughts God has given me over the years and placed them in this book. This book is a compilation of thoughts directly from God, teachings from my leader,

Dr. Bishop Mary L. Alexander, DD., and inspired teachings of great women like Maya Angelou, Iyanla Vanzant, and Oprah Winfrey. This is not the finality of who I am as a women, minister, and woman of God. This is just the beginning.

~ Introduction ~

Chimanada Adiche speaks of the danger of a single story. She tells us that when you reject a part of a story, and realize there is never a single story about any one thing or place, we gain a paradise. This is a wonderful concept and I do not feel that she leaves out the element of God, In understanding the story of an individual or place. The fact is everyone has a story. Some stories come with triumphant sounds of overcoming and some stories come with the dangers of past hurts that never see a state of healing resulting in life, but instead an existent death.

The Bible tells us to die daily. That means every day we must begin anew. We must govern ourselves in forgiveness and seek God for a renewed mind. Our manner of life for seeking God must be continual. Our manner of asking for forgiveness of our sins must be continual. Our manner of renewal in our minds and living a daily Christ-like life must be a daily process. Life changes are inevitable so in these inherent changes we must daily rejuvenate our minds, bodies, and souls.

The word of God helps us gain strength and provides insurmountable knowledge, which aids in our daily fight against the enemy. Satan's job is to take us so far away from God that we believe that God does not exist and we will succumb to living a life without God. Inspiration and feeling empowered is something the people of God need. Most of all, those that have not come into the full knowledge of who God truly is often need support and encouragement.

What does it mean to empower? Is empowerment some entity that seeps in and out of our own realities? Where does it begin? More importantly, where does it have its ending? Is it something that one can create on their own, does it have to be given to you, earned, or inherited. Alternatively, let us try this one on for size. Is it genetic, or is it ingrown in us? It is refreshing when you encounter someone that seemingly has it all put together. They know the right answers to your situation, and they can walk you through your hard times. Something connects to our inner soul where we do not have to question life's circumstances, struggles, or hard moments.

It is my belief that we all have an innate ability for self-empowerment. We all have this innate ability to walk in strength that we can make it through anything. Although some of us are stronger than others, it can be presumed that some of us are taught strength and resiliency from birth. In retrospect, some of us have to work to build that strength and resiliency. It would be nice if it was part of everyone's DNA, but it is not. We have to work to gain this high level of empowerment. Hardships can make it difficult for some to build empowerment, but I believe that we can all accomplish a level of empowerment that helps us maintain in hard times, and celebrate the good times.

So what does it mean to empower? Empower simply means to invest with legal power; authorize. What does empower mean to you? On the other hand, what does it mean to the individuals that have never experienced it, or can find it within themselves right now? If using the previously stated meaning, it means that one has legal power to authorize certain things to happen, certain feelings to arise, and power to allow people, words, or situations to govern how they react.

Simply put we invest in ourselves, or allow others to invest in putting us in a place to feel that we can survive, overcome, and conquer things that happen in our life. In what ways have you been empowered? Has someone taken you under their wings, and aided you in your life's pursuits, heartaches, or trials and tribulations? Take a moment and think about it. Has it always been you forcing yourself to move forward no matter what?

To be empowered suggests there is some daily interaction with some source. Some people use self-help books, some people meet with a mentor, and some people use the word of the living God. Some forms of living an empowered life means that you take a known cliché or excerpt from the late great Maya Angelou or successful Iyanla Vanzant and apply it to your life. I respect both of these wonderful beings, yet one thing at the forefront of their individual and collective ministries is keeping God, In your equation of daily living and empowerment.

This book serves as a history of hurts, pains, overcoming and triumphs and results in statements of daily living that bring empowerment to lives. This book provides its reader with thought provoking quotes that give life to dead situations in which the reader may see no way out. This book is a ministry to pour out the living waters of God's word and nourish the soul of the people. Inspiration and encouraging and how to live a Christ-like life is the ultimate goal of this book.

My overarching theme is that we are all deputies for Christ. We are second in command to ensure that His word reaches the masses. Our lives must be God-balanced and we must ensure that we are living and sacrificing daily to the will of God and what He has for us. He comes to bring life and He wants us to live abundantly.

Every day, my hope is that you will read an excerpt from this book and find a way to be encouraged, inspired, and most of all empowered. I pray that you know that in God, you can overcome and accomplish all that you set out to do naturally and spiritually. This book will serve as a prayer guide for overcoming life circumstances. I pray that it reaches you and those around you. Remember you are a deputy for Christ. Live a God-balanced life and be renewed daily. God bless and enjoy what God has given me for you.

~Spiritual Warfare~

The art of spiritual warfare is essential in the process of prayer. Beyond the aspect of thanking God for all He has done and will do, asking for forgiveness, and placing all your petitions on the altar, you then have to call out the enemy and rebuke his plans, plots, and schemes. You have to be able to speak against the enemy's futile tactics and place division between you and his army. As an ambassador of Christ, we are armed with authority and power over the enemy and his plans. We are armed with strength to lay hold and destroy the works of the enemy. In an effort to do this we are first commissioned to believe in the God we serve and maintain relationship with God, In order to come subject to His guidance.

Having a personal relationship and spiritual connection with God helps us to sustain when trouble comes. God, Is the ultimate sustainer. Confiding in God regarding your deepest hurts, fears, and struggles allows Him to place you in a greater position to hear Him and fight the enemy. In addition, allowing Him to strategically place you in His position and will allows a greater opportunity for spiritual warfare against the wiles of the enemy. Satan is always available and waiting to hijack your thoughts and replace them with feelings of regret, guilt, depression, oppression, failure, and missed opportunities to submit directly to God's will.

Having the ability to fight against the wiles and tactics of the enemy means that you have the skill to manifest the art of spiritual warfare. You are able to stand in the gap for yourself and those around you. You are able to call on the cherubim's and warring angels to take charge over any desolate situation. You can speak life to any dead situation simply because God has given you that right. However, you must first believe. You must have the faith that you can fight the enemy. Lose the fear of the enemy to the deep, give your all to God, speak against the plan of the enemy, bind it, and loose it to the deep never to return.

Remember, in order to enter another realm of spiritual warfare you have to be free of fear. Fear and doubt cannot abide the in presence of the Lord. You must freely submit to His will. Remember that with fear comes torment and plays with your mind. The enemy is an opposer of the Lord and wants to you believe that God, Is not alive; thereby keeping us stagnant in our prayer life.

Learning skillful spiritual warfare takes training. Your training is given to you in the heat of the battle and the furnace of your affliction. In addition, your greatest weapon is prayer and communication with God. In the warrior's Psalm (Ps. 144:1) David blesses the Lord, calls Him his strength, the one who teaches his hands to war, and his fingers to fight. God gives us power in our hands and fingers. How amazing it would be to place your whole self in a position to war against the enemy.

~Important Elements of Worship~

Worship is the act of appreciating God for His nature and worth. It is considered a way of submitting to God and reverencing Him in honor and a sacred personage. In worship, we adore God, In spirit and truth. There are several components to your worship. You first have to rediscover why you worship. Why do you feel your worship is important? How does your worship bring you closer to God? There are distinct patterns that must exist in your worship so that it does not feel mundane and repetitive. You have to delineate which pattern of your worship is real to you or routine.

It is important to have the proper attitude in your worship as well. You want to ensure that you are approaching God, In humility and preparation to hear His voice, guidance, and instruction. Worship must take place in harmony and order. In your worship, you must practice patience. You have to stay in a posture of worship until something happens. Worship is not just about singing or waving your hands. It is about truly acknowledging God, reverencing His awesome power, and inviting His spirit to join you and intercede for you. Worship is about staying there until you surpass that first heaven, join with God, and truly connect to His presence.

Finally, there should be an overall understanding that God, Is worthy of all the praise and our worship.

Some guidelines for worship is to know why you do it (Lev. 7:38). In the Old Testament, they had to make sacrifices of worship in many forms with numerous rituals. That being said, your worship should be a daily ritual. Furthermore, do not ever forget why you worship and do not take it for granted. The way we go before God, Is important. Another component is the element of meditation. Meditation is important because it can help us enjoy the silence of God and worshipping God, In a quiet place is important because it can block out distractions that enable us from hearing Him, while placing us in a position to hear Him clearer.

Our worship should not feel meaningless and should be continual (Num. 28: 1-3). Worship is progressive. The Word says in James 4:8, "Draw nigh to God, and He will draw nigh to you. Cleanse your hands, ye sinners; and purify your hearts, ye double minded." In order for God to get closer to us, we have a responsibility to get closer to Him. Our mind and heart should be clear and pure for sincere worship.

Worship puts us in a place of importance with God because we do not forsake His promises. We must not forget to worship God and we must remember Him in His entire splendor in our worship. Our situations and challenges should not reduce or denigrate our desire or place of worship. Your worship will bring you into God's presence (Ezk. 48:35).

It is important that during your time of prayer, fasting, and worship that worship is free from distractions. True worship cannot be done in chaos, confusion, destruction, or misdirected self-interests. We must love and reverence God unselfishly. God does not selfishly bless us, or selfishly bring us out of our trouble. Our worship must be presented as a genuine sacrifice. It should not feel fake, phony, and full of unemotional, detached, self-reliant, and self-guided knowledge. However, our worship should be in full submission to God for His grace (Jdgs. 17:6). Submission in worship is essential because it is our own choice. It is not something that is forced. We choose to lay prostrate before the Lord and cast our burdens and cares on Him. We choose to allow Him to infuse His love with our burdens and create such a barrier that His presence lifts the burden.

Living a righteous life and conducting yourself with moral actions is also important in worship. When you are outside the will of God and living an unholy life, this can stifle your ability to connect with God, In the spirit. When you worship God, you have to remember your morals and these morals should be consistent with righteous conduct (Ps. 15). Not only should you consider your morals during your time of worship but also the space where you worship (I Kings 7:40-47). In the edifice of the church, the design supports our ability to worship. We have the pulpit to lay in submission and give our burdens to God. We have other "holy" references to support visual aids in our worship.

These aid support to draw our minds in. In our homes, it is important to consider how our environment supports our worship. What elements are conducive to the atmosphere to bring in the Holy Spirit? Do you need music, specific lighting, and candles?

Music is helpful during worship (Ps. 81: 2-4). The use of music can be helpful to draw your mind and emotions in to connect with God. Music can be used to help you meditate on what you are seeking God for or create a balance in the atmosphere for you to effectively lay your burdens down at His feet. Therefore, music and the space you are in should be conducive for worship. In addition, ensure that your space is uncluttered. It does not denote that you have to do major spring-cleaning to go before God. Let us be realistic we do not all have house cleaners that come in and keep every part of our home clean. However, it is essential to attempt to create a prayer place. The movie War Room provided a great example of having a space where you can meet the Lord. A place where you can lay every burden on His proverbial altar, and be free from all distractions.

Your motives during worship are important. Our worship should be free from self-serving needs and should be for the right reasons (II Kings 17: 27-29). We should worship God, In spirit and in truth (John 4:24). You cannot try to abide in worship with the Lord yet continue to straddle the fence between righteous living and disobedience. However, come to God with your true self and in honesty so that He can renew your mind. Our actions and attitudes should be based on God's ability to bring us out. However, to change our actions and attitudes we have to meditate on God's word. His word will change our actions and attitudes and this can counteract with our worship unto Him.

The timing of worship and how often it occurs is important (I Chron. 9:22-32). Worship should not only take place one time per week when we go to the church house. However, we should prepare by worshipping throughout the week. When you create a pattern of worship, it allows an easier process to break through the barriers that the enemy has tried to create for all week.

Preparation is essential. You can prepare for worship by reading the Word, listening to uplifting music, meditating on God's mercy and loving-kindness, speaking directly to God, and thanking Him for His goodness. The reality is that worship should be at the center of your lives just as the heart is at the center of the body. Blood flows through the heart and sustains us to live. Our worship should be a part of our daily lives and we should all the word of God to flow through our minds, bodies, and souls so that we are sustained by God's love, guidance, and connection (I Chron. 9: 33-34). In order to connect with God, seriously requires wholehearted confession.

It is important that confession precede your worship (Neh. 9:2-3). Sin cannot dwell in your worship. God's word, or the reading of it, should precede confession; it helps us understand morally what we should or should be doing. In addition, it helps us understand what we must confess and creates an opening for true worship. We have to go into worship with a sense of purity. God's Word helps us to understand the essence of purity, and how important it to come to Him with a pure heart. God's word is a portal for worship.

Know this, God enjoys our worship and praise; however, it should not feel like a chore (Ps. 122:1). We should always have a good spirit when we come before God. Our everyday can become habitual from work, school, home life, family, church, etc.; however, we will speak of these things with joy. Well, some of us (smiling). Nevertheless, going to work, school, or church, and even taking care of our family is simply out habit. Yes, out of love too. However, we have a pattern of doing it. For some, it is simply their make-up and totally defines them.

Everything we do when it comes to our lives relates to survival and obligation. Why should not our worship be about survival? When we worship it simply has to be something that we equivocally put in the process of our day, and there is an element of obedience and sacrifice that comes along with it. We know that the word tells us that obedience is better than sacrifice. Obedience allows for true reverencing and submission to the Lord.

Your pattern of worship is just as important as the place of worship (Lam. 2:7). This does not mean that you do not assemble yourself. However, it does mean that you do not confine your worship to the four walls of the church. Developing a pattern is important in the sense that it gets us used to the structure of worship, yet it should not be so technical and mechanical. However, if you have a well-developed pattern of worship where you worship should not be a factor. Remember, worship starts at the center of your heart, so it is not subject to a place. We are to carry the Word in our heart, so, in essence, we carry God with us. Because we carry the Word in our heart, and God, Is the Word, we carry His presence. His presence is omnipresent; therefore, your worship counteracts with His presence. You can be in one place, feel God's presence, be in another, and feel God's presence.

Your faith is important in this process. Faith without works is dead, right? So, maintain a good level of faith while seeking God through worship. Your faith can empower God to move on your behalf. God, Is a rewarder to those that diligently seek Him (Heb. 11:6). Do not be weary in well doing when you do not understand the process.

~Beginning Prayer~

Father, in the name of Jesus, You are a wonderful God. You are a merciful God. You are a God full of majesty. You are the Alpha and Omega, the beginning and end. You are the author and finisher of my life. God, you are worthy. I thank you for this opportunity to come before you. I thank you for your loving kindness, mercy, and grace. I appreciate every opportunity you give me to come before you. I do not take these opportunities for granted. Your wisdom and love guide me through every situation, and for that, I am grateful.

God, I appreciate the generous love you bestow on me daily. I thank you for being in the midst of every situation I have. I thank you for the guidance you give me through your Word. God, I ask for forgiveness of my sins, known and unknown. I ask for forgiveness of my thoughts, ways, deeds, and actions that cause me to sin against you. God, please forgive me of any doubt or lack of faith I regard in my heart.

God, every word you have spoken to me is good. God, I ask that you will continue to provide me guidance through my life. I ask that everything you commit to my hands you allow to prosper. I ask that you give me the strength that I need to face every situation in my life, and pursue and conquer my healing.

God, I ask that you heal me from every hurt that I have experienced that holds me back from my purpose. God, I submit my life to you. I submit my past to you. I submit and commit my ways to you, Lord. My life is in your hands.

Lord, help me to forgive those that have hurt me. Help me to forgive those that have taken things away from me in my life. Help me to forgive the actions of those that left me overcome with issues of guilt, feelings of abandonment and neglect. I ask that you help me to forgive those that have taken advantage of me and left me feeling desolate and lonely. God, I ask that you give me the strength to focus on what I need to do to heal and not on what has happened.

I speak against the plans and works of the enemy. I disallow and denounce any works of the enemy and his army. God, I bind in Heaven and Earth, issues of guilt, neglect, frustration, anger, hurt, anguish, low self-esteem, un-accomplishment, doubt, fear, destruction, and anything other diabolical issues resulting from past hurts created by the enemy to destroy mentally, physically, and emotionally. I send everything designed to destroy me back to the depths of Hell never to return.

I loose, in Heaven and Earth, the power and authority given to me by way of Jesus Christ, as an ambassador, the strength to overcome all the issues and circumstances of my past. God, I speak life to every dead situation in my life that I encounter. I declare and decree that I have the power over the plans and works of the enemy and his army. I declare and decree that from this day forth I will begin the work I need to do to conquer my past and work toward my healing.

Today is a day of newness and beginning.
In Jesus' name, Amen.

How to Use this Book

The purpose of this book is to serve as both devotional and journal. The devotional aspect of the book provides instructions on how to get through different aspects of life. The journal aspect of the book provides the reader with an opportunity to work through the healing process of that particular topic. There is an element of poetry throughout the book which serves to enlighten and give strength.

Finally, there are prayers of activation to help you begin praying with a purpose. Every prayer is uniquely tailored to fit a specific area and they give you the strength to begin activating your prayer life in other areas. I do hope you enjoy every aspect of, "Deputy for Christ," and begin the healing process in your life, or simply be encouraged.

Let The

Journey Begin...

~ Taking Action ~

Nehemiah 6:9 "For they all made us afraid, saying, their hands shall be weakened from the work, that it be not done. Now therefore, O God, strengthen my hands."

Taking action requires movement. The birth of success comes out of your passion to do or become someone great. Empowerment is a thought provoking process to see oneself as capable of attaining the goals that are necessary to complete our God-given mission. We all set out to become something or someone great. We all have some sort of goal no matter how minuet. To accomplish the goals we must know when and how to take action. Taking action simply implies that you know what you desire, have laid out your plan, and begun the process to get to the finish line.

It is apparent that during the process we will meet obstacles face to face that may create stagnation. However, we must have an unbroken strength that will keep us pushing forward. When you take action, it means that you have gained momentum to move closer to who you desire to become. One thing we cannot negate is who God has fashioned us to be. We must keep God, In the equation of attaining our goals. *Many are called, but few are chosen*. God expects us to be great in the Earth both spiritually and naturally. We must take the strength out of failure and place our strength in the will of God. To do this we must take action and seek God. Do not just be called to do something great...be something great. Today I choose to be great, fear is not an option.

~Prayer of Activation for Goal-Directed Action~

Father God, in the name of Jesus, I pray today a prayer of activation for taking action over my goals and life. I pray that the fire of God overtakes my life and mind so that I connect with my inner passions, desires, and accomplishments. I speak over my life insurmountable strength that will surpass any obstacle that gets in the way of me accomplishing my goals. I denounce any plan of the Enemy and take authority over his schemes that would keep me from the joys and triumphs God has for me.

Finally, I pray that I will press toward the mark of the higher calling, which is in Christ Jesus. Today is my day of action. I am mentally and physically prepared for victory.

I will take authority over all negativity and pursue peace, God, Is with me.

In Jesus 'name, Amen.

<u>JOURNAL PAGE</u>

Was there a time in which you felt you took action and had a good result?

_____
_____
_____
_____
_____
_____
_____

What areas do you feel you need to take action in your life?

_____
_____
_____
_____
_____
_____
_____

What plans can you make today that will help you and promote you to take action?

_____
_____
_____
_____
_____
_____
_____

~Speaking Life~

Proverbs 15:1-2, A soft answer turneth away wrath; but grievous words stir up anger. The tongue of the wise useth knowledge aright; but the mouth of fools poureth our foolishness.

There is power in our words. We have the power to speak life or death to any given situation. One word can change your whole day or your whole perception of what you see or think. Words have different meanings and when used in certain ways can empower or dehumanize people. As a child grows, it is important to impart positive words in their life. Children that live with scrutiny and discouragement often become scrutinizers and discouragers.

We must ensure that we create of legacy of words that reach out to children and their children that spring forth life. Our words should empower one another and create an atmosphere of love. The Bible says, *with love and kindness have I drawn thee*. It is important to think before you speak. Think about what and how you say things. You can say what you mean and mean what you say, but do not be mean when you say it.

Proverbs 1:28 says, *The heart of the righteous ponders to answer, but the mouth of the wicked pours out evil things.* We must seek God and ask God for help to bridle our tongues. Proverbs also tells us that a *gentle word turns away wrath and harsh words stir up anger.* Watch your words. Speak life to every situation.

Today, I will talk to myself more than I listen to myself. Listening to yourself can create a defeatist attitude when you are not saying the right things. Today speak life to yourself and when yourself speaks back yourself will answer with life.

~*Prayer of Activation for Speaking Life*~

Father God, in the name of Jesus. Today I pray that my words become seasoned words that speak life to every dead situation. I pray that I obtain and maintain the ability to use words to allow the truth of God to manifest in my life. I pray that I not only speak life to myself, but I am able to speak life to those around me. I disallow any plan of the enemy that speaks to me and against what you say. When Satan speaks, I will listen out for you, God.

I pray that I maintain the ability to hear you when you speak.

In Jesus' name, Amen.

JOURNAL PAGE

What areas in your life do you have negative thoughts or conversations about?

_____

_____

_____

_____

How do you feel you can begin to speak positively about situations even when you feel they are negative?

_____

_____

_____

_____

How will speaking positive change your perspective about the negative things that affect you?

_____

_____

_____

_____

How effective you feel in speaking life to situations that make you feel stagnant?

_____

_____

_____

_____

~Having a Constant Faith~

Daniel 3:16-18, Shadrach, Meshach, and Abednego, answered and said to the king, O Nebuchadnezzar, we are not careful to answer thee in this matter. If it be so, our God whom we serve is able to deliver us from the burning fiery furnace, and he will deliver us out of thine hand, O King. But if not, be it known unto thee, O king, that we will not serve thy gods, nor worship the golden image, which thou hast set up.

What happens when we are in the midst of change? Change requires that we have the ability to shift and transition. Not everyone handles change in the same way. During the change process, we must not lose our faith. We must accept the challenge to possess transitional faith. That simply means, that as transition, expected or unexpected, occur, your faith remains constant. Our faith should not decrease when situations suggest we do not have faith. Our faith should increase when we see things decrease. We must refuse to have a stagnant faith. Our mind and bodies are intertwined. Our natural central nervous system must be connected to the nervous system of our faith. This natural and faith believing system has to be connected and in working order. Our faith has to be automatic. To be a faith change agent our brain our heart and blood flow must be synchronized with our mind flow that connects to God. If medication can create change to support our natural nervous system then what more can we ask from the number one doctor who can heal without a pill....it requires belief...faith.

~*Prayer to Activate Constant Faith*~

Father God, in the name of Jesus, today I pray that my faith moves and breathes like the breath of God shifts through my body. I pray that as situations arise that my faith is not moved. I declare and decree over my life that I will maintain the ability to move mountains simply by exercising my faith. I pray that even when I cannot see what God, Is doing that I will maintain a resilient faith. I speak against the enemy that comes to shake my faith and belief in God. I denounce any thoughts or actions that indicate a faithless attitude.

I declare and decree that my faith shall stand firm and be not moved.

In Jesus' name, Amen

<u>JOURNAL PAGE</u>

What areas of your life are you experiencing change that make you lack in your faith?

_____
_____
_____
_____
_____
_____

What does having a consistent faith look like to you?

_____
_____
_____
_____
_____
_____

What thoughts do you feel you have cause you to lack in your faith?

_____
_____
_____
_____
_____
_____

~Listening for God~

Psalm 64:1-2, Hear my voice, O God, in my complaint; Preserve my life from the dread of the enemy. Hide me from the secret counsel of evildoers, From the tumult of those who do iniquity.

The words, "silent," and "listen," have the same letters. You must be silent to listen and listen to learn. Listening requires and implies that there is an intent to follow through with what a person needs from you. God listens to us with intent to fulfill promises He has made for our lives. I once heard a man say, the concept of Deja vu was a conversation God had with us before He sent us here. God sent us here knowing we would call on Him from time to time and KNOWING that He has every intent to hear our cry and supply our needs.

Listening is an important part of prayer. After you pray lay and wait for God to speak. His Holy Spirit intercedes for us. The Holy Spirit utters the prayers even our own heart does not say. Be still and allow God to hear the words or your heart. Yet, pay Him the same courtesy and listen to hear Him when He speaks. Why wait for the world to listen when God's ears are bigger?

~*Prayer of Activation for Listening and Hearing God*~

Father God, in the name of Jesus, today I pray that my ears are open to hear you when you speak. I pray for an open heart to listen to your words and accept the life and energy of what you say. I declare and decree comprehension and retention of everything you speak to me. I encourage myself that I will be able to apply your words to my life and situation. I reverse any negativity from the enemy. I disallow any thoughts from the enemy to seep in and take the place of your thoughts. I command my thoughts to align with the thoughts of God and shift my thinking for greater victories.

God, I trust you and I am listening. Speak directly in my ear so that I may hear your instructions and apply it to my life.

In Jesus' name, Amen.

__Journal Page__

What areas in your life do you feel God listens the most?

_____
_____
_____
_____
_____

How do you feel you put yourself in a position to listen to God?

_____
_____
_____
_____
_____

What process do you take during prayer to ensure that you are listening to God?

_____
_____
_____
_____
_____
_____

~Changing Your Mindset~

Ephesians 4:23-24, "And be renewed in the spirit of your mind." "And that ye put on the new man, which after God, Is created in righteousness and true holiness."

Our mind is a very important part of our being. Our mind holds our memories and can shift our thinking. *What a man thinks so is he,* Proverbs 23:7. What is your mind telling you? What are the constant thoughts in your head? The mind can be a dangerous place when your thoughts become habits and the habits become a part of your everyday life. Do not be so adapted to your situation that you allow maladaptive behaviors to take residence in your life and mind. If you have negative opinions stored in your subconscious, depending on what is being said, your outward conscious needs to speak louder. Begin to counteract maladaptive behaviors and thoughts with positive thoughts and behaviors that are adaptive to positive and Godly living. Change your mind to change your ways.

~*Prayer for Activation to Change your Mindset*~

Father God, in the name of Jesus, today I pray that my mind will align with your thoughts and will for my life. I will activate positive thoughts and be renewed in my mind. I pray for understanding of your ways so that I may live a righteous life. I declare and decree that my thoughts are your thoughts and my ways are your ways.

I rebuke Satan, and bind his plans to make me think on negative things that do not support your will for my life. I reverse negative thoughts and speak positive thoughts so that I may come into the fullness of God's ways. I will only think of the goodness of Jesus Christ and will maintain a mindset of growth, love, encouragement, peace, and joy.

In Jesus' name, Amen.

JOURNAL PAGE

What thoughts do you have in your mind that make you feel inadequate?

_____

_____

_____

_____

_____

_____

What steps do you feel you need to take to work on changing your mindset?

_____

_____

_____

_____

_____

_____

What are some thoughts you used to have that you have changed that make you a better person and give you a better outlook on life?

_____

_____

_____

_____

_____

_____

~Being Shaped in God~

Jeremiah 1:5, "Before I formed thee in the belly I knew thee; and before thou camest forth out of the womb I sanctified thee, and I ordained thee a prophet unto the nations."

My leader provides parents with a poem during baby dedications that states, "Children Learn What They Live." Children are shaped by their environments, by their communities, the choices of parents, and by many other circumstances in life. Many patterns of learned behavior come out of what shapes a person. Some people learn to function out of their issues of abandonment and neglect and never learn to trust. Some function out of hate and their response to life is one of anger.

I am used to some things in life. I am used to some patterns of behavior from others and myself. There has to come a time in which I decide to get passed what others think about me versus what I think of myself? We are programmed to believe what others believe about us, those important to us that is. We are programmed to act out or withdraw when others do not see or acknowledge our capabilities or show us the love we think we need.

Why do you think it's so important to shape children with a mindset that they can accomplish anything they set out to do or that they are beautiful and wonderfully made. People shape people. Children learn what they live.

Don't wait around for people to believe in you, believe in yourself and mix that with the belief that God believes in you and then true shaping begins. Today, I will believe God and I will let God shape me.

~*Prayer to be Shaped and Molded in God*~

Father God, in the name of Jesus, today I pray for your hands to shape and mold me. I pray for a submissive spirit that allows for your spirit to guide and lead me through the process and change so that I become what you called me to be from the foundation of the earth. God, It was you that knew me in my mother's womb, so I ask with your magnificent power that you give me the ability to become a change agent for your glory. Satan, I renounce your plans now to distort my God given shape to shape your negative ways. I govern myself according to God's plan and all things, according to His will, are shaped within me to bring me to an expected end.

In Jesus' name, Amen.

JOURNAL PAGE

What are some learned behaviors or habits you still maintain that keep you from functioning in the capacity of which God has commissioned you to be?

_____
_____
_____
_____
_____

How have the thoughts of people (family, friends, acquaintances, etc.) shaped your thoughts about who you are?

_____
_____
_____
_____
_____

What thoughts do you feel God has about you that can reshape how you think about yourself?

_____
_____
_____
_____
_____
_____

~Inspiration through God~

2 Timothy 3:16-17, "All scripture is inspired by God and profitable through teaching, for reproof, for correction, for training in righteousness." "So that the man of God may be adequate, equipped for every work."

Inspiration is important. We have moments that we are inspired and moments when we inspire someone else. Think back on a time and recollect any moment that inspiration fueled you. Today be an inspiration or allow a moment to inspire you. There is a reason for every moment we have every interaction has meaning. You never know who is going to need your moment. In desperate times, reaching out to someone can mean a world of difference. When you have situations that adversely affect your progression, only surround yourself with those that can inspire you. Simply stated, press forward and inspire someone to be inspired.

~*Prayer of Activation for Inspiration*~

Father God, in the name of Jesus, today I pray that your inspiration will overtake my life and that everything you have allotted to my hands will prosper. I pray that as I reach out to you for guidance that you direct my path. I pray that you will open my mind and heart to what you have for me so that I may become an inspiration and a light to others that have a hunger and thirst for righteousness.

In Jesus' name, Amen

JOURNAL PAGE

What inspires you the most and why?

_____
_____
_____
_____
_____

Who inspires you the most and why?

_____
_____
_____
_____
_____

How do you feel you inspire people? What are some other things could you do to inspire people?

_____
_____
_____
_____
_____

~Commanding Your Day~

Is. 45:11, "Thus saith the Lord, the Holy One of Israel, and his maker, Ask me of things to come concerning my sons, and concerning the work of my hands command ye me."

"Command," means to direct with specific authority or prerogative or to have or exercise authority or control over. There is something wonderful in sustaining the ability to decree and declare what can happen during the course of your day. The enemy already has plans to destroy you. However, when you put yourself in a strategic position to speak against the plans of the enemy you are effectively using the mouthpiece that God has provided us to fight in the atmosphere. The atmosphere is the domain of the enemy. Remember he is the prince and power of the air. Yet, when you stand praying and declaring and decreeing, speaking life to your life it can create a barrier between the enemy's plan and his ability to intercept your prayers.

Command, in your life everything that God promises you daily. Even the enemy cannot stop the promises of God. Declaring and decreeing a thing puts your faith and belief in a position to fight for you. It means that you are free and allowing God to do what He said He will do every day.

Commanding you day is a simple task. It is speaking life to the humdrum and discouraging any tactics and foolery from the enemy.

~Prayer of Activation for Commanding Your Day~

Father God, in the name of Jesus, today I command peace, love, joy, strength, and most of all guidance from the Holy Spirit to take over my day. I command that nothing in me or around me will distract the orchestrated plans made by the hand of God.

God, I ask that your spirit guide me in my words and actions today as I go about work and other tasks.

In Jesus' name, Amen.

<u>JOURNAL PAGE</u>

How do you command your day?

_____
_____
_____
_____
_____

What is your response to things when situations come along to create chaos in your day?

_____
_____
_____
_____
_____

The enemy's job is steal, kill, and destroy. How are you making daily plans to avoid the schemes of the enemy?

_____
_____
_____
_____
_____

~*Positive Conversations and Interactions*~

Phil. 1:27, "Only let your conversation be as sit becometh the gospel of Christ: that whether I come and see you or else be absent, I may hear of your affairs, that ye stand fast in one spirit, with one mind striving together for the faith of the gospel."

In every decision or conversation you have remember to always seek God first. Asking God to guide your words and bridle your tongue in the most eloquent fashion can mean the difference between the life and death of a situation or conversation. I, often times, find myself praying right in the midst of someone talking and asking God to guide my words. I find myself asking God to give me the right words to say right in that situation. If the person needs peace, I ask God for a peaceful way of stating something. If a person needs guidance, I ask God to give me the instruction He wants them to have.

In seeking God, whether in conversation or mere interaction, we are allowing ourselves to come subject to a divine orchestration by God. I believe there is a purpose for every interaction. I also believe that from every interaction we should learn something spiritually and naturally about ourselves. The problem is we do not take the time to ask God what we should say. We base interactions off our own emotions and experiences. In doing this, you can give the wrong advice. The fact of the matter is that God provides instruction. It is important to ask His Holy Spirit to guide you and lead you in every interaction so that you are in alignment with what He has to give you and the other person.

The enemy is waiting for you to speak negatively to someone's pain or agony. He may not expect you to speak life. So be aware of the tactic of the enemy that comes to bring negativity to a situation. The disclaimer is to remember that the enemy may be lurking in the mist of your situation, but even the mist evaporates. Hear God, speak clearly, and seek God with a clear mind.

~Prayer for Activation for Hearing God Before you Speak~

Father God, in the name of Jesus, I thank you for giving me the opportunity to come before once again. God, I present myself a living sacrifice that is humble and open to hear your words. God, I ask for guidance as I go in this conversation or interaction with one of your children. I ask that you guide my words. I ask for an active listening ear to be able to hear what the person has to say. I ask that you provide me with divine instruction.

God, I bind the plan of the enemy that comes to intercept what is good in this conversation and manipulate it for his own plans. I loose in the atmosphere a one of one connection with this individual that result in respect and consideration.

Father I pray, that at the end of this encounter that your will, will have taken place and the life of the person I have this interaction with is changed.

In Jesus' name, Amen.

JOURNAL PAGE

If you could put your negative talk on a scale from 1-10; how would you rate how often you speak negative?

_____
_____
_____
_____
_____

On your job or in ministry what situations do you discuss more that make you feel negative?

_____
_____
_____
_____
_____

Provide two positive options you could have for avoiding engaging in negative conversations.

_____
_____
_____
_____
_____
_____

~Anticipation for God~

Ps. 27:4, "One thing have I desired of the Lord, that will I seek after; that I may dwell in the house of the lord all the days of my life, to behold the beauty of the Lord, and to enquire in his temple."

When you anticipate being in the Lord's presence that is an indicator of your confidence in His abilities to meet you, hear, and deliver. God, Is ready and willing to serve your needs. He is your light, your salvation, and strength. You need only to wait on Him. Have courage and draw closer to Him. It is one thing to look forward to situations in our lives that bring celebration. However, every day we should work to celebrate with God for the things that He continues to do in our lives. God, Is a present help in the time of trouble. He is a giver of peace. He is waiting for you. We should wait for Him and show excitement when He shows up.

Having butterflies is not always an indicator of anxiety for something or another whether it be good or bad. However, that feeling is the Holy Spirit connecting to your human elements indicating that something is brewing showing that God, Is present and waiting for you to say I need you. Having the anticipation to meet up with God, In prayer and praise allows for a better connection with Him. *Today, my mind spirit and body is free to connect with God. God......you give me butterflies.*

~Prayer of Activation for Anticipation of God~

Father, in the name of Jesus, you are such a worthy God. You are a present help in the time of trouble. You make the crooked ways straight. God, you are my strength and you are my salvation. I am grateful that you allow me to come before daily. I look to seek your face. God as I abide in you, I ask that you abide in me. God as I draw closer to you, I ask that you draw closer to me. God, as I seek your face, help me to grow in you and stay connected to you.

I pray against the plan and works of the enemy. I disallow the works of the enemy that would come along to bring distraction and change my thoughts and mind. God, I ask that you give me the strength and wherewithal to not compromise my position. I submit my body as a living sacrifice and will seek you with joy and anticipation of your greatness.

In Jesus' name, Amen.

<u>JOURNAL PAGE</u>

What areas in your relationship with God excite you the most?

_____
_____
_____
_____
_____
_____

What are some things you do to connect with God to show Him that you are excited about being in His presence?

_____
_____
_____
_____
_____
_____

What areas can you improve on to show God that you are waiting and desire to be in His presence?

_____
_____
_____
_____
_____
_____
_____

~Overcoming Adversity~

Ecc. 7: 13, "Consider the work of God: for who can make that straight, which he hath made crooked?"

Facing adversity is a necessary part of life. Adversity helps us to learn patience, and practice the elements of perseverance. Adversity, if handled correctly, can teach us how to maintain a sense of integrity and character. Adversity can leave with a sense of hopelessness, which, if not handled with prayer and sound spiritual guidance can lead to disruptions in your daily functioning. The best part about this is you get an opportunity to show God that you trust Him. It is one thing to be happy during times of prosperity; however, it is another to sustain your trust and belief in God during times of adversity.

Although some situations are bearable, there are some situations that come along to show you where your weaknesses lie. Some things show that you are broken and some things show you that you have insurmountable strength. Some things make you want to look for a way out or seek peace and solitude. Some things happen and lead to chaos and confusion. The one *SOME THING* I am sure of is that my Savior is real. I am sure that in this *SOME THING*, God will boost me, dry my tears, heal my pain, and immobilize and generate my natural and spiritual man to rise and be better.

Although some things are warranted God gives us a lifetime warranty.

~*Prayer of Activation for Overcoming Adversity*~

Father, in the name of Jesus, I thank you for allowing me another opportunity to come before. You are worthy and greatly to be praised. God, you are my strength and I appreciate you for all that you do, have done, and will do in my life. Father you are the Alpha and Omega, the beginning and end. You know all things. You know what I stand in need of. You know the outcome of my situation. Only you can keep me from falling. You, Lord, provide the necessary steps for me to come out victoriously. God, you are my refuge and my strong tower.

Father, as I seek your face, help me in my time of need. God show me where I error, and Lord provide with me with the wisdom I need to get through my time of adversity. God, I cannot make it without your help. I need you Lord. Satan, I bind your works and plans that come along to distract me and cause me to feel hopeless. I bind and lose to the deep any form of depression and oppression. Father, I declare and decree that you will give me the strength to stand against the wiles of the enemy. You said no weapon formed against me shall prosper. Father, help me to endure, because in this I know that you will have the final say.

In Jesus' name, Amen.

65 | P a g e

<u>JOURNAL PAGE</u>

What adversity or challenges do you face that cause barriers between your prayer life and relationship with God?

_____
_____
_____
_____
_____
_____

How do you feel these barriers keep you from having a successful prayer life?

_____
_____
_____
_____
_____
_____

What steps are you willing to take to change how you respond to your adversities?

_____
_____
_____
_____
_____
_____

~ *Caring for Others* ~

Galatians 6:2, "Bear ye one another's burdens, and so fulfil the law of Christ."

Alan Deutschman, states, "The act of caring ultimately instills the emotion of care." Have you really showed someone you cared about them? Caring for someone can be shown in different forms. Some people may not ever say with words that they care about you. However, they may show that they care for you in their actions. When I was young in Christ, I found it difficult to believe that He cared for me. My thought pattern was, "If you cared for me why would or should I have to go through such challenging times. If you, Christ, cared for me why did I have to be raped or molested, or abandoned?"

In my eyes, if Christ did not care about me then who would? Caring was always a measurable fact for me. If I did not see it, then you did not care. If you did not say it, then you did not care.

Ironically, I spent the majority of my life making sure that people knew that I cared about them. I wanted to be helpful. I tried to be a good listener if you need someone to talk to. When you called, I would be right there. I wanted to believe that I was a great helper to many. I wanted those in my life to know without any doubt I cared for them.

Caring for others should not be daunting tasks. For some it comes easy. The reality is that we should all recognize our ability to serve and care for others. Your ability to show someone you care allows you to connect with Christ. Christ cared for all he came into contact with. He cared for those that did not even exist. Caring is a learned behavior. Caring is something that is taught by those around us. Children learn to care at an early age.

Today is RAOC DAY –Random Acts Of Care. Show someone you care today, then share, and post your experiences on my page and yours to encourage and uplift your neighbor. Pay your care forward. This is a challenge.

~Prayer of Activation for Caring for Others~

Father God, in the name of Jesus, you are precious in my sight. God, I thank you for every opportunity that you give me. I thank you for the opportunities that you give me as a willing vessel to care for people. God, please give me the ability to speak life to every situation of any individual that I come in contact with on today. Help me to have the knowledge and wisdom on how to care for people that need to feel you kindness and love on today. God, help me to be willing and open to help those and guide them in any area that needs support. I speak against the plans of the enemy that will come to cause distractions when I am helping someone. I speak against the barriers the enemy will try to cause to happen so that I miss any chance of caring for or helping someone. God, I decree and declare that the wisdom that you have placed in me will help me to care for others.

In Jesus' name, Amen.

JOURNAL PAGE

How do you feel you care for others that you come in contact with?

_____
_____
_____
_____
_____
_____

How do you feel God prepares you to care for others in your ministry, job, family, etc.?

_____
_____
_____
_____
_____
_____

What areas do you feel you need to improve on when coming in contact with people that need your help?

_____
_____
_____
_____
_____
_____

~A Part of God's Army~

~2Tim. 2:3, "Thou therefore endure hardness, as a good soldier of Jesus Christ."

An army is defined as a large body of people organized and trained for land warfare. God used armies in the Old Testament to destroy, bring order, and support those that sought Him for favor to overcome their enemies. To understand the concept of battling you have to understand the concept of war and what we war against. The Word explains, *"For we do not wrestle against flesh and blood, but against the rulers, against the authorities, against the cosmic powers over this present darkness, against the spiritual forces of evil in the heavenly places."* Our ability to be part of God's army means to understand that the battle we fight is not always visible to us. We fight against every dark thing the enemy tries to put in our way to distract us.

To be in the army of the Lord you have to understand the propensity of serving the Lord. The battle is not yours it is the Lord's. In 2 Chronicles, 20:15, the Word says "And he said, Hearken, ye, all Judah, and ye inhabitants of Jerusalem, and thou king Jehoshaphat, Thus saith the Lord unto you, Be not afraid or dismayed by reason of this great multitude; for the battle is not your, but God's. Once you understand that the battle is not yours and you do not have to fight it, you become a true soldier. When we, soldiers for the Lord, fight we do it in prayer, worship, and praise. The mentality of the Lord's army has to be one of endurance, patience, faith, and belief.

Alan Deutschman (Change or Die) states that the gang's mentality is based on vengeance. A gang is an army that wages war against other gangs to keep their turf safe and protected. The tactic of this gang, or army, is retaliation and control. Being a part of a particular gang gives you a reputation of fear and power. The amazing thing about being a part of God's gang (army) is the power that He places in each and every one of us to overcome the struggles of this life. The war that the enemy wages against us is one of control and instillation of fear. In retrospect, we do not have to war with the enemy because the war is in God's hands; we only have to be obedient soldiers and watch God overcome for us.

I am a part of gang...a gang of believers and our mentality is based on God. God's Gang, and your initiation...kill the enemy.

~Prayer for Activation for Being a Member of God's Army~

Father God, in the name of Jesus, I thank you God for you are awesome. God, you continue to make ways out of no way. You make the crooked ways straight and continue to reveal your majestic power in my life. God, you are great and greatly to be praised.

God, I ask that you give me the wisdom and knowledge to be an effective member of your army. Give me the faith, patience, and belief that I need to know when to move out of the way and allow you to war for me. God help me to stand strong against the wiles of the enemy. I pray against the plans and works of the enemy. I bind the works and plans of the enemy that come to wage war against me. I pray against and denounce all sanctions of the enemy that make me an ineffective member of your army. I decree and declare that I have the strength to stand against the tactics of the enemy and that I am an effective soldier in the army of the Lord.

In Jesus' name, Amen.

<u>JOURNAL PAGE</u>

How do you define being a soldier in the army of the Lord?

_____
_____
_____
_____
_____
_____

What attributes do you feel you have that make you an effective member of God's army?

_____
_____
_____
_____
_____
_____

What areas do you feel you lack in being a part of God's army?

_____
_____
_____
_____
_____
_____

~Overcoming Negative Experiences~

Heb. 10:35, "Cast not away therefore your confidence, which hath great recompense of reward."

In most cases, negative experiences shape our view of people and the world around us. Negative experiences shape our ability to trust and believe in what people say or do. Negative experiences cause depression and oppression. In addition, negative experiences that are not worked through with some degree of healing, keep us stifled and unable to tap into the full promises of God. These negative experiences if not worked through, govern how we manage our world. It will govern how we raise our children as well. I struggled in my life with trust. Because of negative experiences and issues of abandonment, my mindset was, "Do not get too close because everyone leaves."

Unfortunately, feeling like everyone leaves kept me in a waiting place for the moment when the person actually left.

I never allowed myself to feel anything. When I did feel something, I later realized it was a false perception of an overwhelming desire to be loved. My reality was that people do not really love you like they say they do. Unfortunately, this shaped my relationships, friendships, and other ongoing interactions. Trying to balance out that feeling of not wanting to experience anything negative and love unconditionally.

The reality is we have to work hard to overcome negative experiences. Some people can simply move passed a situation without worry. On to the next, in most cases. Some of us dwell on the hurt or pain of a situation, which makes it hard to shift our thinking to a positive mindset. Our own choices cause this negative pattern and keep us from growing individually.

You may not possess the ability to undo horrible things you have said or done. You certainly cannot undo what someone else has said or done to you. However, you do sustain the ability to do so many good things that the scale will begin to tip (Silbert). Tip your scale today no matter what someone thinks or what you think about yourself or things you have said or done. Do not let anyone or even yourself hold you hostage to what has been. Forgive yourself move on and balance out the good you have done with more good. Hold onto your faith and exercise with the belief that God, no matter what, has you in the palm of His hand.

~Prayer for activation for overcoming negative experiences~

Father God, in the name of Jesus, you are so wonderful. You are present and willing to give me opportunities to come before you with a humble heart and full of thanksgiving. God, no matter what has happened to me you have been

ANDREA M. DAVIS

consistently supporting me and loving me. God, I thank you for your presence in my life.

Father, I pray for forgiveness for those that have hurt me. I pray that you will have mercy on them. Father, I ask for forgiveness for any hurts that I have caused myself. God, I ask for the ability to be steadfast and unmovable ever abounding in your works. I pray that you give me the ability to see beyond my past experiences and failures as your way of preparing me to minister to those that need your word.

God, help me not to limit myself and my abilities that you have placed in my by focusing on past hurts. God, I use the authority that you have placed in me to denounce and dismantle the plans of the enemy. I speak against his desire to leave me in a broken place. I decree and declare that on this day I will have life in every situation. I speak that from this day forth nothing from my past experiences shall haunt me. I decree and declare that your light will shine through me.

In Jesus' name, Amen.

Note: No matter what has happened in your past you have to move towards forgiveness for yourself and the people that have caused you pain. This is an important step in healing and activating your ability to hold on to God's unchanging hand.

~Poets Corner~

He Makes Me an Overcomer

Overcoming fears, no more drowning in my
tears.
Waves of life like six feet high
Consuming my world, not enough to keep me
from drawing nye.
Nye to the Lord, He's my source
He is my help, He is my living water
I will call to Him
I will seek Him
He makes my way broader
He makes me an overcomer

I cannot imagine this life now being consumed
by my fears
When he tells me I am a conqueror year after
year
Verse after verse with the passages of time
My God, Is worthy
He is yours, He is mine.
I am an overcomer

JOURNAL PAGE

What are some negative experiences that continue to influence how you govern yourself today?

_____
_____
_____
_____
_____
_____

How do you feel you can begin to work towards forgiveness of yourself and others?

_____
_____
_____
_____
_____

Name three things from your past that keep you stagnant in your faith. How do you plan to work towards overcoming these issues?

_____
_____
_____
_____
_____
_____

~*Living a Christ-Like Life*~

I John 3:2, "Beloved, now are we the sons of God, and it doth not yet appear what we shall be: but we know that, when he shall appear, we shall be like him; for we shall see him as he is."

Today I imagined what I would do if the rapture came and I was left behind. The first thing I thought to do was race to my home and school to see if my kids were gone. Although I would be sorrowful I would rejoice in the fact that I taught them well and they carried the spirit of the Lord with them until the end. That they set an example for their peers and lived an anointed life. I then thought of the time I would have to go over in my mind what I could have done better, what I could have said better or how I could have lived more of a life that exemplified Christ. What kept me from rising in the sky to meet Christ? Teach your children so that when that day comes you will be together with Christ. Live everyday as if it is the rapture. What would your rapture thought be?

Sometimes we think because we go to church, sit in the first pew, yell, and scream out scriptures that we are Christ-like. We think because we treat everyone right, smile when we do not feel like it, do not curse or have sex out of marriage, we do all these great things so we are Christ-like. Characteristics associated with Christ are prayerful, wise, faithful, virtuous, obedient, patient, charitable, giving, and forgiving. These are just to name a few. However, the basic premise is to practice these attributes in our daily living.

This can be hard when you come across people and situations that can easily take you out of character. Our human side wants to lash out at people and let them know a thing or two with some choice words. We want to give up and throw in the towel. We cannot see or understand what God, Is doing in our lives and some just do not see the need for growth in their lives. Living a Christ-like life means that you have to live beyond what you feel sometimes. You have to appreciate a person despite their negative ways. I have learned and I am still learning to be consistent no matter what. This is not an easy task. However, when you put your faith in God and you seek Him in everything you do, He will guide you and direct your path with the wisdom of how to live according to His will and live a consistent Christ-like life.

~*Prayer of Activation for Living a Christ-Like Life*~

Father, in the name of Jesus, you are a wonderful God. You are a god of provision and a giver of life. You make all ways straight and provide guidance to me in everything I do. Each day you give me life is another day to live like Christ. It is another day to be a helper, to show forth gratitude with a humble attitude, to care for those that are sick and heavy laid. God, I thank you for the opportunity to make another choice to live according to your word. I appreciate you every day. God, I ask that you help me to continue to be humble like Christ. God, help me to be kind to people. Help me, Lord, not to succumb to the worries of this world and become the world. However, Lord help me to exceed pass the problems of this world and use the ability you placed in me to be a light for those that do not know you or simply need your help. Help me to be an example of a true Christian and work towards immolating Christ.

Father, I speak against the plans of the enemy that come along to take me out of character. I decree and declare that you, Father, will be in the midst of every interaction that I have and show me how to work as a true servant like Christ.

In Jesus' name, Amen.

~*Poets Corner*~

I Want to Be Like Christ

I want to be like Christ
A great deal of patience, love, and wisdom
I want to be like Christ
I want to experience spiritual freedom
Being like Christ is no easy game
Especially if you're doing for only fortune or
fame
This don't come with no money, this don't
come with no prestige
However, you can only do this if you are able
to see the need
God, Isn't human He's not like you or I
He walks in place you cannot only source of
healing when you cry
Being like Christ means you have to get
beyond yourself
Get beyond the pain of your past, you have to
leave it on the shelf
Not to dwell on or go back to, because Christ
do not deal with our past
He works in the forward, especially if yesterday
was not your last

I want to be like Christ
My life depends on only Him
I need Him daily because this life can be so
grim
But to have His character the strength that He
bore

Not to treat my success in Him like a game
that has been scored

Christ was not a failure
He gave his life for me
He did it for you to, why be like anyone else
honestly
Being like Christ means that my heart is just
that easy to mold
Be like Christ now and watch the mystery of
His love unfold.

<u>JOURNAL PAGE</u>

What areas do you feel you exemplify Christ-like behaviors?

_____
_____
_____
_____
_____
_____

What areas do you feel you need growth in?

_____
_____
_____
_____
_____

What are some changes you can make to demonstrate growth in those areas?

_____
_____
_____
_____
_____

~ God's Time is Not Your Time ~

Patience is Key

Hebrews 10: 36, "For ye have need of patience, that, after ye have done the will of God, ye might receive the promise."

When going through, we often question, "How much longer do I have to go through this specific thing?"

We wonder when God, Is going to shift things so we are not uncomfortable with what is taking place. Our patience wears thin and we struggle to hold onto our faith. We learn very young, to wait and have patience. However, this is not a task that is perfected in childhood. We have to wait for many things. We have to wait to grow in ministry, we have to wait to get the job we want, we have to wait on our jobs to be recognized, we have to wait. Waiting develops our character. It is in your waiting where you learn to stand on God's promises. It is in the waiting where you learn to persevere and see God for who He truly is.

The point is to understand God's timing. His timing is not our timing. God knows when to strategically place you in the position to receive the blessing He has preordained for your life. It is important not to move out of God's timing. When you move out of His timing you disrupt the will He has for you because you are now living according to your own will. You should never view your waiting as time wasted. Time is never wasted although moments make you feel that way….time is exactly what it is…time…it's gone when it's gone. Use your time wisely. When you feel you are down for the count, wait and be patient, God will help you get back up.

~*Prayer of Activation for Having Patience*~

Father, in the name of Jesus, You are truly a wonderful God. I thank you for making provisions for me in my daily life. Your love for me is a daily indicator that you trust me. I ask that when situations arise that can stifle me and cause me to become distracted that you will give me the strength to wait on you. I pray that you will give me the power to stand and hold onto to your promises. Lord, I know that your promises are yay and amen. I ask that while I wait patiently on you, that you increase my endurance and perseverance. I bind the works of the enemy that come to feed my mind with negative thoughts. I loose peace in my mind and spirit, and the strength to know that Your unchanging hand is moving things in my favor.

In Jesus' name, Amen.

~Poets Corner~

Waiting on God

Timing is everything
But patience is the key
Time and patience can only exist
Where the heart and mind agree

I want things when I want it
I need what I want to come now
God why do you make me wait
Why can't we just be on the same page?
You're not hearing me Lord
I can't wait for things to change

I can't keeping waiting for you yes
I feel like I'm about to explode
I'm crying I'm yelling hear me out loud

Can't you see my pain?
This waiting game, I've had enough
God do it right now, because this wait is too
rough

Please open the doors of heaven and poor out
my blessing
You said command ye me
I'm in place, I'm trying to be like you, can't
you see

I deserve this blessing, I deserve the change
at this moment

Come on Lord I need you, where are you I'm
waiting

Ah, I get it, you need me to trust you while I
wait
When I trust you, you'll come to me and let me
know the fate
Of this situation, but in my waiting I'll grow
If I wait on you, with patience, you'll reveal
what I need to know.

<u>JOURNAL PAGE</u>

How would you rate your level of patience on a scale of 1-10, 10 being a great amount of patience and why?

_____
_____
_____
_____
_____
_____

What areas of your life has it been frustrating to wait for God to move?

_____
_____
_____
_____
_____
_____

How can you begin to practice patience?

_____
_____
_____
_____
_____
_____

~Accepting God's Love vs. Man's Love~

John 3:16, "For God so loved the world that He gave His only begotten Son, that whosoever believeth in him should not perish, but have everlasting life."

There is a distinct difference from someone hugging you rather than someone knowing you need to be held and holding you. Connection is important. God loves us with a special love. His love is unchangeable, inseparable, and sacrificial. God loved us so much that clothed Himself in flesh so that He could live among us and ultimately die for us. The love of man cannot transcend boundaries. The love of man cannot protect you like God's love. God's love is consuming. We expect love from our parents and other family members. We expect love from individuals that we are in relationships with. When that love does not come the way we want, it can inadvertently shape us. It shapes how we interact with others that come in our lives.

Sometimes we focus so much on wanting man's love that we deny ourselves the ability to accept God's love. God loves us, but He is waiting for us to *accept* His love. Sometimes it is hard to accept God's love because we do not love ourselves. We have made mistakes or things have happened to us that make us question love from anyone, even God. We may ask, "Why do you love me so much and I keep making the same mistakes over and over? Why would God love me and I keep sinning and making choices that keep me away from God?"

It's because God's love does not have boundaries like man's love. Man's love says, "If you do this, I will love you. If you love me this way, then I will love you this way."

God's love is simply what it is. He loves us with a special unchanging love.

~Prayer of Activation for Accepting God's Love~

Father, in the name of Jesus, you are a wonderful God. You sent your son to die for me, and my soul salvation. I thank you for your lovingkindness and mercy towards me. Father, I thank you because you love me even when I do not love myself. When I doubt you and lack in my faith, you still love. God, your love is precious and I thank you for it. Father, please help me every day to accept the love that you have for me. God, help me to love myself despite any choice that I have made. Father, cover me in your precious blood and heal me from the hurts that cause me to question your love for my life.

God, I bind the plans and works of the enemy that comes to make me question your love for me. I speak against and denounce every worker of iniquity that tries to bring a spirit of disbelief and doubt in my mind. I decree and declare that my thoughts and ways are aligned with you God and that I am in complete connection with the love you have for me.

In Jesus' name, Amen.

~Poets Corner~

He don't love you like I do

My love is different
My love don't discourage you
Or make you feel bad about yourself
My love doesn't harbor resentment
My love can't fail you
My love doesn't die
My love doesn't consume you, then leave
hanging out to dry
He don't love you like I do

My love won't miss a beat on how to make
your heart feel happy
My love won't treat your love messed up and
crappy
My love is not just for a moment until you get
what you want
My life is precious to Him; He wants me to
accept His love
I truly want to love me back
He don't love you like I do

My love gives you peace
His love gives you joy
I won't take it away from you, and treat you
like a toy
My love is unconditional
It speaks to the whole of your being
My love is never ending
He don't love you like I do

Even when you turn your back
Even when you sin and give up
My love is still there
My love never fails
He won't love you

Journal Page

Do you honestly feel that God's love you? Why or why not?

_____

_____

_____

_____

_____

_____

Name at least 3-4 people you feel love you unconditionally.

_____

_____

_____

_____

_____

_____

Do you love yourself?

_____

_____

_____

_____

_____

~Maintaining Your Character In Christ~

Prov. 22:1, "A good name is to be chosen rather than great riches, and favor is better than silver or gold."

Your character is very important. People will know you based on your character. People will tell others about you based on your character. In some cases, people hear about your character before they even meet you. I often say to someone I meet for the first time, that says, "I've heard a lot about you," all good things I hope. The reality is, if I am living a life exemplified by Christ, treating people right, demonstrating "good" behavior in all facets of my life, then I should not have to hope it is good or not. I should know it is good because of my character I display. This is important and listen well. This display of character happens outside the four walls of the church.

One of my life lessons in developing my character was the way I talked to people. I had then tendency to be very swift with my mouth. I really did not have a filter. At one point, long ago, I asked God to help me to be meeker in my approach with people. Unfortunately, that did not work for me to its full advantage. However, I still have to learn when the Spirit says, "Stop! Before your mouth takes over to stop EVEN!!"

When my buttons are being pushed. I had to make a decision not to focus on what the other person was doing or saying, however, I had to focus on my response to the person. Moreover, I had to focus on how I was going to leave that person feeling and how that could determine my character with others.

Maintaining character in God, Is knowing when you should step away. It is knowing when you need to take a break and reevaluate, not the other person, but yourself. I will continue to work on not allowing people to take me out of character and listen to God when He says, "This is about to get ugly you know you and so do I."
Practice silence even when you want to fight verbally. Be silent let insults fly by and keep your sight on who God knows you are and beware of our words that kill when you are trying to kill someone else. Keep your character about you despite people so you're in a good place with God. Know in what areas you need growth to grow your character in God.

~Prayer of activation for Maintaining Character Christ~

Father God, in the name of Jesus. You are so worthy of all the praise. You are the creator of all things. You make all things new. You are wonderful and I appreciate you for all you do. God, I thank you because I know that if I follow your laws you will continue to bless me. God, I thank you for every opportunity you give me.

God, I ask that as I seek you, you help me to display a Christ-like character to those I come into contact with. God, I ask that every encounter I have you be in the midst. God, you give me the words to say.

God, help me not to become easily frustrated and taken out of character when dealing with negative situations. God, I speak against the enemy that tries to create situations that may take me out of character. I speak to those issues in me that are unresolved and may rise up in me and denounce anything that is unlike you God. I decree and declare that the Holy Spirit will guide my actions and my response to people. I decree and declare that I will maintain a positive character

In Jesus' name, Amen.

Note: Character is who you are, whether it is good or bad. It should not be mistaken for integrity, which is the state of being undivided. It is who you are when no one is looking. Your character is surface and what everyone sees.

~Poets Corner~

Who Did You Say You Are?

Who did you say you are
I can't tell one day from the next
You change like the winds
Your changes got me vexed
Come on now for real
One day you nice and sweet
The next time I see you
You acting like some chick off the street
Who did you say you are?

Get your mind right
Get it together
Decide who you want to be
Going back and forth with you is getting crazy
You say you like Christ
You think like He think
You act like He act
You say you like Christ
But is that really a fact

Your character is undivided
Don't get it confused with integrity
When the doors are closed
What will people say to me
About who you are and what you propose to
portray
Consistent with your character
Night or day
What would Christ say, about who you say you
are?

What would Christ Say?
Don't let your character be a falling star
Who are you again?

JOURNAL PAGE

What do you think most people would say about you behind closed doors?

_____
_____
_____
_____
_____
_____

What characteristics do you think you have that match the characteristics of Christ?

_____
_____
_____
_____
_____
_____

What areas of your character do you feel you need to improve on?

_____
_____
_____
_____
_____
_____

~ Productivity and Perseverance = Success in God ~

Ecc. 7:8, "Better is the end of a thing than the beginning thereof: and the patient in spirit is better than the proud in spirit."

I have always been a person that if you tell me what I cannot do I work to prove you wrong. I never felt I was smart enough because of comments that were made to me as a child. I never accepted that I was smart enough even though I graduated high school with a 3.64 GPA. I received my bachelors and master's degree – yet, I still did not feel that I measured up in intelligence to my peers. The point is I never stop trying. I had a goal to become a psychologist and I was going to reach that goal. When I put my mind to something there is not stopping me. I want to be successful so I was going to put in the work. Circumstances came, some by my own hand, that caused a delay in my blessing, but I kept pressing.

Productivity is essential to whatever goal you are trying to accomplish. If you do not do the work then how do you accomplish what you set out to do? Setbacks are going to occur undoubtedly. Anything worth working for will not come easy. I am thankful for the things that have not come to me easy because it has taught me perseverance, to maintain a tenacious attitude that hard work pays off, and in the end that it is all worth it. I refuse to be a person that gives up because things do not happen the way I like. I hang in there and press forward. Whether it be a place, relationship, or spiritual goal I won't give in, I won't give up, I will win. If that thing, relationship, or spiritual pursuit is out of line with God's purpose then I will be productive in seeking God so that I remain aligned with His will. Productivity produces. Work and do not stop until God, Is done.

God gave man dominion over the earth and earth. It is well within our reach to accomplish our goals. We were purposed to be fruitful within the earth. Everything you touch and everywhere you walk is blessed. Success is already established for us we just have to tap into it and never give up.

~Prayer for Activation for Productivity and Perseverance~

Father, in the name of Jesus, you are such a loving God. You have given me the resources that I need to be successful and conquer my goals. You have given me the victory over my enemies and even over the enemy in me that can keep me stagnant. God, you have blessed me daily and I do not take your blessings for granted. God, forgive me for any doubt I place on you or myself. God, help me to become successful in whatever I plan to do with my life. God help me to be in alignment with you.

Help me not to waiver in my faith. God provide me with the guidance as I acknowledge you. I speak against and bind the plans of the enemy. No weapon formed against me shall prosper. I decree and declare that God has given me the tools to be successful. I decree and declare that I will not give up, but stay in the face of God and do the work that God has commissioned me to do. I am a conqueror and no thing shall keep me from accomplishing all the goals I set out to do. In Jesus' name, Amen.

Note: You cannot accomplish the goal if you do not set out to do it. Here are a few steps to start working towards your goal.

1. First, in all things, pray and thank God. Pray for the wisdom you need to start moving towards accomplishing your goal.
2. Write down what you want to do. The Bible tells us to write the vision and make it plain. What do you see yourself doing? What are you good at?
3. Decide how you need to accomplish your goal. Do you have to go back to school? Do you have to get some additional training?
4. Do a search for the programming/training you will need to accomplish your goal.
5. Write down any barriers you feel you face that will keep you from accomplishing your goal. Recognize that I said barriers you feel you face. I said that because what is a barrier to you is not a barrier to

God. Satan creates barriers to keep us stagnant. These barriers can be crossed.

6. Make phone calls and go to these schools or agencies in person that can help you move towards accomplishing your goal. If people do not know you need the help, then how can they help?

7. Do not be afraid to hear the word no. Know this, a no is not always the final answer.

8. Every problem or barrier has a solution. Figure out the solution and continue to create avenues so that you are not stuck.

9. Do not GET STUCK! Keep moving and keep the words, "I can't," out of your vocabulary. Keep pushing and telling yourself that giving up is NOT an option.

10. In all things be thankful and trust that God will bring you to an expected end.

God's commitment to you exceeds your commitment to yourself. God wants to see you successful.

Journal Page

Write down goals you set out to accomplish and have not yet completed.

_____

_____

_____

_____

_____

_____

What circumstances have stopped you from moving forward with your goals?

_____

_____

_____

_____

_____

Where do you see yourself in the next five years with accomplishing these goals?

_____

_____

_____

_____

_____

_____

~Focusing on the Good in Others~

2 Samuel 1:17, "And David lamented with this lamentation over Saul and over Johnathan his son,"

When David learned of Saul's death, he chose to highlight all the good Saul did rather focus on his inconsistencies. This took courage. There were times when individuals around David wanted him to kill Saul when he had the chance. David respected the kingship Saul was given by God. David did not let the negative things Saul did govern how he entreated Saul even in death. Sometimes people are not going to make the best decisions and they may not always treat you right. I believe that if those individuals are only going to focus on your faults, then let them go. Remember, you cannot change people, but you can change their interaction with you by how you interact with them. Take time focusing on the good in people.

This can be a daunting task for some of us. It can be difficult to see the good in people when you are automatically programmed to see the bad. You do not trust what they say. You definitely do not believe what comes out of their mouth. In order to focus on the good in people, you have to recognize the issues within yourself that cause you to only see what you believe is negative.

Sometimes our past hurts only allow us to see the negative side of people. We are so far gone, that we cannot see. Some of us have been hurt and when a situation is remotely similar to something that has hurt you before, then you put your guard up and cannot see pass your hurt.

There are times that people do things and others want to make them suffer for their choice forever. All the while, this person has forgiven himself or herself, asked you for forgiveness and you refuse to recognize their positive choices. If you are constantly waiting for the bottom to drop and only see the negative side of a person, then you make it difficult for people to develop positive relationships with you. The big part of this is you can put a strain on your relationship with God, because God wants us to see the good in others.

~Prayer of Activation for Focusing on the Good in Others~

Father God, in the name of Jesus, I thank you for loving me for who I am. I appreciate that you love me beyond what I can imagine. I thank you for not turning your back on me when I was not doing all that I know I should do. God, I thank you that you look beyond my faults. God, I praise you and honor you in all things. God, I ask that you will continue to help me to see the good in others. I ask that in every situation I encounter that you allow me to see passed my own issues and selfishness to see the good in others. I pray that my vision is aligned with your vision and that you help me to visualize the good in people despite what my natural eye may see.

God, I block the plans of the enemy that come to make me have a contrite heart toward my fellow brother or sister. I pray against and disallow distractions that come to cause dissention and distort my vision of what a person's heart truly is. God, I decree and declare that I have the ability to maintain a positive relationship with those around me. I pray for the ability to trust and see the good in people despite what my past situations cause me to see. God, I thank you in advance for the ability to love people without boundaries.

In Jesus' name, Amen.

<u>JOURNAL PAGE</u>

What are some of your inward issues that cause you to avoid trusting the good in others?

_____
_____
_____
_____
_____
_____

What areas do you feel you need to conquer to help you see passed what you perceive is negative in others?

_____
_____
_____
_____
_____
_____

How can you begin to do your own healing so that you are in a position to see the good in others?

_____
_____
_____
_____
_____
_____

~ Recognizing the Inward and Outward Enemy ~

2 Corinthians 4:16, "For which cause we faint not; but though our outward man perish, yet the inward man is renewed day by day."

The enemy seduces us into believing that our insecurities are our realities. He makes our inconsistencies look appealing to us, and we support or participate in this seduction by falling subject to our thoughts and actions that totally negate God's purpose for us. This causes an inward battle that we do not have to fight. If God says the battle is not yours, it is His, then that means that any battle, inward or outward, we do not have to fight.

It is sad when the enemy pits us against one another. It is equally sad when the enemy uses things inside *us* that we refuse to recognize or we just do not know is there, to pit us against those that love and cherish us. Satan will use different tactics to create distractions and disruptions within us and with those around us. Speak boldly and directly to Satan, saying, "Satan, I see what you are doing but know this! God has the final say and no matter what happens, God will still prevail because you have not taken hold of my soul or those around me."

~Prayer of Activation for Renewal of Your Inward Man~

Father, in the name of Jesus, today I pray that you will continue the work in my life. I pray that you will deliver me from those things in me that cause distractions and disruptions. I pray against the wiles and schemes of the enemy that uses what I see as an inconsistency. I pray that as I abide in you, my inward man is renewed daily.

Lord, help me to ensure that my flesh is not a distraction that keeps me from getting closer to you. God, increase my discernment to see when the enemy is trying to trap me in my past issues, and give me the strength to hold onto your unchanging hand.

In Jesus' name, I pray, Amen.

<u>JOURNAL PAGE</u>

What are some of your inward battles?

_____
_____
_____
_____
_____
_____

What is the issue you fight with the most?

_____
_____
_____
_____
_____
_____

How do you typically handle this issue?

_____
_____
_____
_____
_____
_____

~Maintaining a Stable Faith~

Heb. 10:36, "For ye have need of patience, that, after ye have done the will of God, ye might receive the promise."

Having faith in God, at some point, becomes easy for the believer. However, the danger in not having faith in oneself can shake the faith you have in God. If you begin to believe that you will not conquer, then you begin to lose faith that God has made you a conqueror. If you begin to lose faith that you can accomplish all that you set out to do and that it is impossible, then you lose faith that God can do the impossible. If you begin to lose faith in your confidence, then you lose faith that God, Is your confidence. Our natural faith in our own abilities has to be connected to our faith that we have in God. Today, my faith that I have in God will be connected to the faith I have in myself. I will subdue and conquer. I will accomplish all I set out to do. Now faith, stable faith, assured faith, God, Is my faith.

Faith and unbelief cannot dwell in the same place. You cannot waiver and say that you have faith, and yet have unbelief that God can bring you out. Maintaining a stable faith means that even when discouraging circumstances come along you still have faith. It means that even when no one believes in you and where God, Is taking you, you still have faith. It means that you no longer look at your circumstances as obstacles, but you see them as stepping stones to get closer to what you are trying to do. You have to get to a point where your faith does not hold hands with regret, guilt, or issues from your past. Your faith has hands and feet, and walks you through every dead situation in your life and causes you to have seen life in it.

Note: Today become a master of your faith and let God work. Maintaining your faith is something that you consistently have to work at. God will not give you faith, it is simply there for you. You either have faith, do not have it, or you allow the enemy to make you waiver in your faith. Do not give strength to the enemy but questioning God and renouncing your faith. Be consistent and hold onto your faith.

~*Prayer of Activation for Maintaining a Stable Faith*~

Father, in the name of Jesus, You are a sovereign God. You are the only true and wise God. You are the only god that can sustain me. Only you can me from falling. God, you are a way maker, a healer. God, I thank you for everything. I thank for being a provider, my deliverer, my joy. God, you are awesome. God, please forgive me of my doubt. Please forgive me when I lack in my faith. God, be with me through every situation. Help me to maintain my faith. God, as I go about my day please give me the strength to depend solely on you. God, I break the strongholds of the enemy that will come to shake my faith. God, I speak against and denounce the works of the enemy in my home, on my job, or wherever I go.

God, today, I decree and declare that my faith is stable. God, I decree and declare that I trust you in everything I do and my faith cannot be taken away from me.

In Jesus' name, Amen.

JOURNAL PAGE

What areas of your faith do you feel you lack the most?

_____
_____
_____
_____
_____
_____

What areas do you feel are more stable?

_____
_____
_____
_____
_____
_____

Relate one situation in which you maintained your faith? How did it work for you?

_____
_____
_____
_____
_____
_____

~*Patience and Praise*~

Heb. 13:15, "By him therefore let us offer the sacrifice of praise to God continually, that is, the fruit of our lips giving thanks to his name."

We come to church every week and praise God and dance all over the floor. We dance over issues from the past, present, and fret over the future. We dance for form or fashion. Some dance because it looks good. Some dance because it is simply part of the process. Praising God feels good. Praising God can lift the heavy burdens. Praising God can give you just enough energy and strength to get through to the next week. The caveat is that our praise should not be ritualistic in nature. We should do this continually and unto to God as a reasonable service of thanksgiving.

In the process of praising God, there must be an element or potion of patience. If we are praising Him in and out of season or in advance for something, then we know that we are praising Him for things that have not yet come to past. So our patient praise must be a symbol and dance of faith in which we know that what God has said and promised will come to fruition.

If our praise includes an element of patience, then we are able to maintain our praise because patience means you have the ability to wait for what you want or need without wavering. You maintain your strength. You ensuring that you are not giving up. In addition, you do not succumb to throwing in the towel. Today, practice patience while not losing your praise.

~*Prayer of Activation for Patience and Praise*~

Father God, in the name of Jesus, you are such a patient God. You are worthy of all the praise. You make ways out of no way. You keep me daily even when I do not pray to you for protection. You love me with an overwhelming love. You keep me even from myself. You understand me when I question why I have to wait. Father, forgive me for doubting. Forgive me Lord, for my impatience. God, forgive me lacking in my trust. God, as I stand before you, help me Lord to be more patient. Help me not to waiver in my trust and have a sustainable praise. God, help me to hear your voice and instruction when I am in a situation where I have to practice patience. God, in every situation help me to remember to thank you and give you all praise, glory and honor. God, I disallow the tactics, wiles, and schemes of the enemy that come to bring me strife and stifle my praise. I speak against the plans of the enemy that come to disrupt my patient.

Father, help me to wait patiently and praise you in thanksgiving without wavering. God, I decree and declare that I am able to wait with patience. I decree and declare that my praise will be consistent. God, I thank you in advance for the wait, because in this I know that I have the victory.

In Jesus' name, Amen.

<u>JOURNAL PAGE</u>

Name one situation in which you feel you did not exhibit patience?

_____
_____
_____
_____
_____
_____

How did that work out for you?

_____
_____
_____
_____
_____
_____

Why do you feel praise is important?

_____
_____
_____
_____
_____
_____

~Not Being Fooled by the Enemy~

Ps. 64:1, "Hear my voice, O God, in my prayer; preserve my life from fear of the enemy."

The enemy seduces us into believing that our insecurities are over realities. He makes our inconsistencies look appealing to us, and we support or participate in this seduction by falling subject to our thoughts and actions that totally negate God's purpose for us. We must open our eyes and command our senses to line up with the affections of God.

The art of seduction requires the essence of human emotion. We must align our emotions with the interconnections of God's heart. The enemy entices us with evil devices and subjects us to a life of enslaved sin. We must abort his plan, and become enticed by God's word and unconditional love he has for us.

I was sound asleep one night and in a dream out of nowhere I was awakened by this evil laugh. I knew it was the enemy. It was a laugh of, "You think you got it all together, but I got something for you."

I immediately began to pray. I told God, "You said, you have not given me the spirit of fear, but of power, and of love, and a sound mind."

I called on the cherubim and warring angels to fight for me in the atmosphere and I denounced every emotion, fear, thought that did not align with the word of God.

We have been given the power to speak against and defeat the enemy. Tap into the power that God has given you. Satan may have laughed that night, but I'm 100% sure got the last laugh.

~Prayer of Activation for Not Being Fooled by the Enemy~

Father God, in the name of Jesus. You are an awesome God. Father I thank you for your power. I thank you for your majestic ways. I thank you for your ability to come to tend to all my needs. I thank you for even when I am weary you are there. God, I praise your name and give you all the glory. God, please forgive me of my doubt. God, please forgive me where I lack in my faith. God, please forgive me when I give the enemy reign over my emotions and situations. Father, please give me spiritual vision to see when the enemy is playing on my emotions. Father, please give me the wisdom to speak against and denounce all his plans. I bind the plans and works of the enemy that comes to cause me to be disillusioned by his tricks and schemes. I loose in Earth and Heaven, the wisdom and knowledge to fight and overcome the enemy. God, I decree and declare that I will not be fooled by the enemy. I decree and declare that the curse will be sent back to the sender. I decree and declare your power and might will overtake me to overtake the enemy.

In Jesus' name, Amen.

~ Poets Corner ~

Don't be fooled

The enemy plays you for a fool
He's conniving at best
He's definitely on his job
Only solace is for those who rest
In God that is

Where are you resting your prayers?
When the enemy comes in
When the flood rushes in
When life over takes you
When you feel like you can't make
Up your mind because the enemy is there
Nagging in your thoughts making you think your
way is fine

You cannot make it
Not even being on your grind

He says I'm waiting for you to give up
You'll lose your mind in this
I got you right where I need you
Why don't you seek me in the midst?

The enemy has got you fooled
Wake up and look to Jesus
He's your only hope

Don't be fooled

JOURNAL PAGE

What are some areas you feel the enemy plays games with your mind?

_____
_____
_____
_____
_____
_____

Why do you think it is easy for the enemy to get in your mind and thoughts?

_____
_____
_____
_____
_____
_____

What tactics do you feel you can use on the enemy to avoid his schemes?

_____
_____
_____
_____
_____
_____

ANDREA M. DAVIS

~Confidence in Our Leaders~

2 Kings 2:16, "and they said unto him, Behold now, there be with thy servants fifty strong men; let them go, we pray thee, and seek they master: let peradventure the spirit of the Lord hath taken him up, and cast him upon some mountain, or into some valley. And he said, Ye shall not send."

Sometimes, you have to leave people to their own devices. People, no matter what you say or do, or what advice you give are going to do what they want. It is as the leaders of the ministry stand before the people every week and give us skills and strategy on how to defeat the enemy, they give us instruction and prepare us with warning to avoid the situations that leave us in defeat. And, we still leave out the same way holding onto our own truth and belief that our situation has not changed. We cannot see that God, Is a God of provision and will supply our needs because we hold onto the false perception of our own desires that keep us safe, yet open to the enemy.

In 2 Kings, 2:16-18, the prophets, although knowing that the mantle fell on Elisha still didn't believe and encouraged Elisha to send a certain amount of men into the mountain and valley to look for Elijah. He told them, "No," initially, and they kept pressing and he then said, "Go then."

They returned and he said, "I told you not to go."

I feel that there was a lack of confidence in Elisha who now held the mantle. We have to trust our leaders to do what they are commissioned to do. We have to be able to take instruction and feedback without putting our own emotions in the way because it can cause hindrance. Finally, when you are encouraged not to do something, as warning comes before destruction, listen and take heed. Elisha maintained integrity because all he said was, "I told you to go not."

There was nothing else to be said. When we are given instruction, we cannot blame our leaders when things do not go our way because we are led by our own selfish desires and do things our own way.

~Prayer of Activation for Having Confidence in Your Leaders~

Father God, in the name of Jesus, I pray over my leader today, that you will continue to make provision for them. I pray that as they guide and lead me according to your statutes, that you will continue to bless them. I pray for a humble heart and spirit as I take heed to their instruction. I ask that you will allow me to have humble spirit and open mind to what my leader has to say. I pray against, and disallow, any tactic from the enemy that comes to bring distraction. I bind the plans of the enemy that will create barriers in the relationship I have with my leader.

Father, as I sit at the feet of my leader, renew my mind and heart. Help me to lay hold to the vision of my leader and be connected to fully understand what is being imparted in me by your chosen shepherd.

In Jesus' name, Amen.

JOURNAL PAGE

What do you feel are important elements of being a leader in the church?

_____
_____
_____
_____
_____
_____

How do you work to develop relationship with your church leaders?

_____
_____
_____
_____
_____
_____

How do you show your leader that they can trust you with their vision?

_____
_____
_____
_____
_____
_____

~Overcoming and Healing from Abuse~

Luke 6:28 "Bless them that curse you, and pray for them which despitefully use you."

Abuse affects so many people. Some people are able to come out of it and become a sounding board for others. Some are overcome by issues of guilt, anger, hurt, frustration, and other impounding issues, so much that we are left in a sea of un-forgiveness. Issues of abuse can govern how you manage relationships, and interact with people. Furthermore, your response or lack of healing from abusive situations effects how you respond to different situations.

Overcoming the effects of abuse is a process. It is not something that can happen overnight. It requires patience, perseverance, and the ability to forgive. It also requires prayer and a direct connection with God. It is essential to understand the root of oppression and depression that comes out of the abuse. So many things have to be rebuilt out of issues of abuse such as trust, ability to maintain relationships, and freeing oneself from strongholds that leave you feeling lifeless.

On the other hand, overcoming abuse and working through the healing process can result in a number of failed relationships. Failed relationships happen out of our desire to have a relationship that makes sense. We desire to be loved the right way. We desire to be treated the right way. We desire so, that we place ourselves in unloving relationships with men, women, and family members because we hope that they will love us right. We are fooling ourselves if we think that the true identity of love will flourish when we do not take the time to heal and love ourselves. True healing from abuse happens when you are able to forgive, face your issues, and live in the present with a positive outlook and perseverance.

~Prayer for Activation for Overcoming and Healing from Abuse~

Father God, in the name of Jesus, you are a holy God. You, God, desire for us to learn how to forgive. God, you love us unconditionally and forgive us for our sins. God, you are wonderful and surely a mighty God. God, I thank you for allowing me this opportunity to stand before. Lord, I humbly seek you for forgiveness of my sins. God, I thank you and believe that as I pray you are working on my heart. God, I am able to forgive because you have forgiven me. God, I ask that you help to deal with the residue of my abuse. Help me to forgive my perpetrators. Help me, Lord, to understand that forgiveness is not for the other person, but it is for me. God, allow me to heal from the issues of my abuse.

Satan, I bind your works and plans that come to take me off balance mentally, physically, and emotionally. I denounce any and all residue resulting from the abuse I suffered. Satan, I am no longer bound to the effects of what my abusers did.

I decree and declare that I am able to forgive. I decree and declare that I am able to maintain positive relationships. I decree and declare that nothing from my past abuse will affect my future plans or ministry. I decree and declare that I am able to walk in total healing. I am free from the stigma of my abuse mentally, physically, and emotionally.

In Jesus' name, Amen.

JOURNAL PAGE

What areas do you feel you need to address to begin the healing process from your abuse?

_____
_____
_____
_____
_____
_____

What feelings do you still harbor toward your abuser that keep you from working toward the process of forgiveness?

_____
_____
_____
_____
_____
_____

What areas of your life do you feel have become stagnant due to your lack of overcoming in this area?

_____
_____
_____
_____
_____
_____

~Poets Corner~

I Was a Child

I was a child
But you decided I was ready to be a woman
You decided I was ready for a woman's choice
You touched in an innocent place
You decided for me, I was a child
I was a child
Subjected to a place that should only be sacred
between a man and wife
You took from me that day, happiness, and
added strife
I was child
Why did you, how could you
I did not know I could say no

I blamed you for stolen innocence
I blamed you for my failures
I blamed you for my hurts and inability to
travail over anything that would stop me from
having a normal life

I hated you so much
I hated anything any person that resembled
who you are and what you did
I blamed you for making me hate

With forgiveness
I can thank you
For giving me my voice
I thank and forgive you
Because I now know that I have a choice

I can live in unforgivness
But that will change what occurred
Between a man and child
Yes, it is absurd

But I do forgive
I was a child without a voice
Now I am a woman of God with a choice

I choose to forgive

~Ending Prayer~

Father God, in the name of Jesus, You are such a wonderful, powerful, and mighty God. You are the Alpha and Omega, the beginning and end. You are the author and finisher of my life. God, you are worthy and greatly to be praised. God, I praise your name. I praise you for your creation. I praise you for being my confidant and friend. I praise you because when I acknowledge you, you are always there to direct my path. I praise and thank you for deliverance and restoration. God, you are a wonderful and mighty. God, you are wise. You are a provider and supplier of all my needs. You are a yoke breaker, a burden lifter, and supreme revitalizer. God, you are merciful and gracious. I thank you for your wisdom on every journey. God, I thank you every time you have lifted me up and out of my depression and oppression. God, you are truly a sustainer.

God, please forgive me of my sins, known and unknown. Forgive me of my thoughts, ways, deeds, and actions that cause me to sin against you. God, please forgive me because I waiver in my faith. Forgive me for doubting you, whether conscious or subconsciously. God, forgive me for the times that I have tried to do things my way and did not seek you first. God, forgive me everything that I do that causes me to deny you full submission.

Father, as I have begun this journey of healing, I ask that you continue to cover me with your love in the process. Help me to understand the process. Help me to understand that everything may not be alright right away, but God, if I stay in you, I will surely overcome. God, I ask that you provide me with every resource spiritually and naturally that will allow me to progress through my healing process. Help me to get closer to you Lord. Help me to not become distracted by the plans and works of the enemy as I go through my journey of healing.

I bind the plans and works of the enemy in the name of Jesus. I disallow and denounce every plan the enemy has to bring distractions to take me off course in my healing process. I loose his evil ways and plans to the confines of Hell and create a barrier so they never return.

Father, I decree and declare that my life is yours. My healing is in your hands. You alone are the ultimate healer. I know that I am healed because through you all things are possible. I am a deputy for you, Lord, and will do the necessary work to speak life for myself and others.

In Jesus' name, Amen.

About the Author

 Andrea is the CEO and founder of Life Movement Empowering Ministries, L.L.C. LMEM, LLC serves to empower women, men, children, and families. LMEM was developed out of Andrea's desire to serve individuals that desire to do better and progress through life, but seem to remain stagnant. LMEM teaches people to progressively move through life, set and accomplish goals, and live life with an empowered mindset. She holds a Bachelor's degree in Psychology from Delaware State University. She completed her Master's degree in Social Work at Widener University where she received a scholarship for academic excellence. She is currently pursuing her Doctorate in Psychology with a specialization in Mental Health Administration and anticipates graduating in 2016. She is the mother of five children, Ayvori, E'lisia, Patrisha, Gabriel, and Delsyn. She encourages her children to make positive life choices and live life refusing to let anything stop them from accomplishing their goals.